Left to Write

GW01458265

Left to Write is a book of photocopy masters providing ideas and exercises for practice in writing. Most students who are not confident at reading or spelling are usually reluctant writers. The worksheets in this book are designed to encourage students at all levels by giving them definite starting points and, in many cases, requiring only a few words or sentences to be written. The range of exercises should make students aware of the different styles of everyday writing and give plenty of opportunities for trying them out.

The worksheets are arranged in an approximate order of difficulty for ease of access. It is not intended that students should work through the sheets in the given order, nor do they have to tackle all of a worksheet. Many of the sheets have a lot of work in them and students should choose items which appeal to them. It is hoped that tutors will find the book a source of ideas which they can adapt to suit their own students. The Index *(p. 48)* gives more detailed guidance to topics covered.

Left to Write is suitable for work at Entry Level of the Adult Literacy Core Curriculum and the equivalent levels in the National Curriculum, although many of the worksheets are likely to be useful at other levels.

Second edition

In this **Second edition** of *Left to Write* there are minor revisions of the text and some updating of photographs and other illustrations, where necessary.

Please read the copyright / photocopying restrictions below.

COPYRIGHT / PHOTOCOPYING RESTRICTIONS

Purchasers may photocopy *Left to Write* for use *within their own centre or single college/school site.* We ask you to respect this permission and not to allow copies to be transferred to other colleges, schools, sites or centres. A tutor who purchases a personal copy may use *Left to Write* on more than one site, provided that they restrict its use to the classes they personally teach and do not allow copies to be passed to other tutors and students. Items from *Left to Write* may not be reproduced in magazines, newsletters, books or on computer disk/tape without the prior permission of the publishers.

Publishers: Brown and Brown,
               Keeper's Cottage,
               Westward,
               Wigton
               Cumbria CA7 8NQ
               Tel. 016973 42915

Copyright   © Hugh and Margaret Brown 1996 & 2004

All rights reserved.

Photocopying is permitted subject to the restrictions detailed on page 1.

If you would like to receive our catalogue of publications for teaching reading, spelling, writing and basic maths, please contact:
Brown and Brown Publishing, Keeper's Cottage, Westward, Wigton, Cumbria CA7 8NQ
Tel. 016973 42915

First published 1996
Reprinted 1999, 2001

Second edition 2004

ISBN 1 904874 03 7

Printed by Reed's Ltd., Penrith, Cumbria on 100% recycled paper and card.

Contents

Finish the sentence (1)

1. He opened the door and ....

2. She said she had met him ....

3. Next year, I will ....

4. The postman opened the gate and a dog ....

5. It was nearly midnight and snowing hard when I ....

6. He was standing at the check-out in Morrison's when ....

7. When I got the package home ....

8. There was a loud bang ....

9. She ran down the stairs ....

10. The old man in the pub looked up and ....

Finish the sentence (2)

1.   He was so angry that ....

2.   I had fallen asleep ....

3.   The kids were on their way to school when ....

4.   The prisoner heard the door clang shut ....

5.   The girl in the Housing Benefit Office ....

6.   The truck driver was just about to ....

7.   She heard a voice behind her say, " ....

8.   As he came into the straight for the last time ....

9.   We are writing to you to ....

10. The cabinet minister got to her feet ....

11. The trouble with this exercise is ....

Put one word in a sentence (1)

Write 10 sentences, each containing one of these words:

1. Pounds

2. This

3. Key

4. All

5. Daughter

6. Street

7. Please

8. Mountain

9. How

10. Seven

Put one word in a sentence (2)

Write 10 sentences, each containing one of these words:

1. File

2. Black

3. Bill

4. Telephone

5. Multiply

6. Italy

7. Lead

8. Because

9. Of

10. A

Add a beginning (1)

1.   .... on the left-hand side, next to the church.

2.   .... at half past four.

3.   .... and some heavy showers.

4.   .... has seen better days.

5.   .... in extra time.

6.   .... jeans and Reebok trainers.

7.   .... Canterbury, Kent.

8.   .... in an old people's home.

9.   .... all over the world.

10.   .... within 14 days.

Add a beginning (2)

1.   .... and a box of matches.

2.   .... into his eyes.

3.   .... the famous film actress.

4.   .... to get there.

5.   .... plastic bag from Kwiksave.

6.   .... for over 10 minutes.

7.   .... as quickly as I can.

8.   .... more than £5.

9.   .... on a DVD.

10. .... but I wouldn't if I were you.

What are they thinking ?

Fill in the thought balloons in the cartoon and photograph below.

What's the answer ?

Make up answers to these questions. Each answer must contain at least 6 words, but it need not be a complete sentence.

1. Where did you get that T-shirt ?

2. When will my order arrive ?

3. How long does it take to get to Belfast ?

4. Who was it I saw you with last night ?

5. Which do you think would be the best one ?

6. When will you be going there next ?

7. Where can I get it repaired ?

8. Why did you choose that colour ?

9. Is it really worth paying an extra £12 for this one ?

10. Is there anything worth watching on telly tonight ?

11. What on earth shall I tell him when he rings up ?

12. Have you any idea what happened ?

13. Did you get my message last week ?

14. Will you be in tomorrow morning ?

What's the question ?

Here are the answers to some questions. Write down what each question might have been.

1. No, I watched the film on Channel 4.

2. Outside Marks & Spencer's at a quarter to ten.

3. It fell off the back of a lorry.

4. At a rough estimate, it will cost between £120 and £150.

5. Just round the corner on the left-hand side.

6. 1st class will cost 60p and second class 47p.

7. 11.20 and then every hour at twenty past until 6.20.

8. He phoned me last night.

9. On the top shelf of the display cabinet over there.

10. She got the bronze medal.

11. She had a baby girl last week and they're calling her Jessica.

12. You must be joking !

13. Two years on probation and a fine of £200.

14. Yes, I will be.

Ask a question and answer it (1)

Make up some questions which begin with these words, then write an answer of at least 3 words to each question. The answer need not be a complete sentence.

1.   How ....

2.   Who ....

3.   Where ....

4.   Why ....

5.   What ....

6.   Which ....

7.   When ....

8.   Could ....

9.   Are ....

10.   Do ....

Ask a question and answer it (2)

Make up some questions which begin with these words, then write an answer of at least 6 words to each question. The answer need not be a complete sentence.

1. Would ....

2. Is ....

3. Please ....

4. Have ....

5. Will ....

6. I ....

7. You ....

8. If ....

9. Did ....

10. Can ....

What are they saying ?

Fill in the speech balloons in this cartoon.

Fill in the speech balloons in this cartoon and add some more graffiti.

Keeping a diary

*Diaries are usually written in note form (**i.e.** not in complete sentences). Write a diary entry of at least 10 words every day for a week.*

Monday	
Tuesday	
Wednesday	
Thursday	
Friday	
Saturday	
Sunday	

Where's the fire ?

Write answers to these questions about the photograph above.

1.   Have the fire brigade just started tackling the incident or are they packing up afterwards ?

2.   Has there been a fire ?

3.   What may have caused the trouble ?

4.   Have you ever had to call the fire brigade ? What happened ?

5.   Write a short news item of no more than 5 sentences about the incident in the photograph. Add a headline.

One sound - two spellings (1)

The pairs of words listed below sound the same but they have a different spelling and meaning. Write a sentence which contains each pair of words.

e.g.   ***heel*** / ***heal***   *The blister on her **heel** was beginning to **heal** at last.*

1.   hear   here

2.   site   sight

3.   wood   would

4.   mail   male

5.   threw   through

6.   by   buy

7.   hole   whole

8.   new   knew

9.   fair   fare

10. week   weak

One sound - two spellings (2)

The pairs of words listed below sound the same but have a different spelling and meaning. Write a short paragraph which contains each pair of words.

e.g.   sore / saw   *The man **saw** the accident happen. He ran to phone for an ambulance. As he rushed back to help the victims, he tripped and ended up in hospital with a very **sore** head.*

1.   of   off

2.   find   fined

3.   pole   poll

4.   been   bean

5.   draw   drawer

6.   know   no

7.   plain   plane

8.   past   passed

9.   it's   its

10.   floor   flaw

Use the same spelling pattern

For each of these boxes, write a short paragraph which contains all the words in the box. Add more words with the same spelling pattern if you can.

ea

eat	tea	meat	seat
bean	near	sea	cream

ck

brick	back	stick	slack
knock	track	rock	lock

ai

rain	pain	again	faint
brain	main	drain	train

tt

better	little	flatter	kitten
bottle	letter	getting	cotton

ee

need	feel	see	week
free	been	beer	meet

sh

show	shift	sharp	she
shoe	shine	shape	should

ou

our	pound	about	foul
doubt	lout	found	proud

le

middle	cycle	whistle	idle
double	puzzle	fiddle	struggle

What happened next ? (1)

Read each piece, then write down what happened next and give the piece a title.

1.

A man was walking home after a night out at the pub with the darts team. He was turning the corner into his own street when he was knocked to the ground by someone rushing in the opposite direction. As he staggered to his feet, he heard a dog bark, the screech of brakes and a high-pitched scream ....

2.

Claire got home from school earlier than usual. Her mother wasn't in, all the doors were locked and there was no note saying where she had gone ....

3.

It was 8.55 a.m. The coach was due to leave at 9 o'clock to take the team to their away match in Doncaster. Two of them were always late.

" There's Jimmy, coming out of the Gents," shouted the manager, " But where on earth is Ryan ? " ....

4.

She'd had a lousy day. She had only been in charge there for 2 weeks but she knew that she was going to have to sort out the sales manager. He obviously had a problem working for a woman. She sat thinking for a while about what to do. Then she picked up the 'phone and called him ....

5.

I was due in Court at 11 o'clock. Although I had been to court many times before, I was worried about how this case would go. My evidence could be the most important part of the trial. I had thought about what happened over and over again but when you get up there in the witness box your mind can go completely blank ....

What happened next ? (2)

Read each piece, then write down what happened next and give the piece a title.

1.

There were just 2 laps to go in the Commonwealth Games 5000 metres. Darren was lying 3rd. There were two Kenyans in front of him and the Canadian champion was on his shoulder. He knew he didn't have the fastest finish, so he had to make his move ....

2.

She had finished her training and it was her first full day on the Customer Services desk. The 'phone rang. She picked it up and, in a bright, cheerful voice, she said:

" South Coast Water. Sharon speaking. How may I help you ? "

The old woman at the other end of the line said: ....

3.

100 feet up in the air, in the cab of the crane, he could see most of the city stretched out in the sunshine. The foreman signalled to him to lift the steel beams. The wind was gusting, so he raised the beams slowly and began to swing them round towards the eighth floor where the gang was working. Without warning ....

4.

They had planned this day weeks ago. The kids had gone off to their Gran's and they were staying with her overnight. The sun was shining and they had the whole day to themselves ....

5.

The waiting room at the surgery was half empty. The morning session was nearly over. A young mum was flicking through a magazine while keeping an eye on her 3-year-old son. He was tottering towards an old man in the corner who was smiling and holding out a sweet for him. Suddenly, the door to the doctor's room crashed open and the young doctor staggered out with a face as white as a sheet ....

You're joking

A. *Write down a joke which begins:*

1. Doctor, doctor ....

2. Knock, knock ....

3. Have you heard the one about ....

4. Waiter, waiter ....

5. What's the difference between ....

6. What do you call a ....

7. Why do ....

B. *Write down your own favourite joke.*

Writing notes (1)

Write short notes of at least 10 words for each of these situations:

1. Wife telling husband what there is to eat when he gets home.

2. Daughter telling father where she's going for the evening, so that he can pick her up afterwards.

3. Saying why a child can't go to school.

4. Secretary passing on an urgent 'phone call for the boss from an angry customer.

5. Girl telling her boyfriend why she wants to stop seeing him.

6. Warning a colleague at work about a breakdown or fault on a piece of machinery.

7. Making a shopping list for yourself to remind you which shops you want to go to as well as the items you want to buy.

8. Making a check-list of things to do before going on holiday.

9. Giving directions for someone to get to your house.

10. Your grandmother, who is hard of hearing, has taken down a 'phone message about when someone is coming to repair the washing machine. Write what the message says.

Writing notes (2)

Write short notes of at least 20 words for each of these situations:

1. Giving directions for someone to get to your local secondary school.

2. Taking down a message recorded on an answerphone at a mail order firm from a customer who wants to be sent a catalogue.

3. Making a check-list that a best man might write for himself before a wedding.

4. Explaining to the service engineer what has gone wrong with your central heating boiler.

5. Office trainee passing on a personal 'phone message to the boss from someone in the family.

6. Leaving a note under the windscreen wiper of a car in a car park.

7. Arranging with a friend about meeting them for a night out.

8. Your brother is on holiday abroad and you have been keeping an eye on his flat. You discover a break-in one day. Make a list of all the things you need to do about it.

9. The council is proposing to knock down half of your street to put a new road through it. Write down a few notes to remind you of the main points you want to raise at the public meeting tonight.

10. You have to give a short speech at work about a member of staff who is retiring. He has been there 23 years. He hasn't been very well liked and everyone is really quite pleased to see him go, but you have to be polite. Write some notes to remind you what to say.

How do you do that ?

Write down instructions for someone else on how to do any of the tasks below.

    1.   Use a public telephone.

    2.   Fill up a car with petrol.

    3.   Sew a button on to a shirt.

    4.   Buy a ticket for the National Lottery.

    5.   Cash a giro cheque, a postal order or a pension.

    6.   Record a radio programme on a minidisc.

    7.   Cook a frozen pizza in an oven or a microwave.

    8.   Paint a new door.

    9.   Put a new electric plug on to a vacuum cleaner.

  10.   Iron a shirt.

  11.   Find the soccer results on Teletext.

  12.   Photocopy something in a public library.

  13.   Use the washing machine in a launderette.

  14.   Set a video recorder to record a TV programme.

One word - two meanings (1)

For each of these words, make up a sentence which contains the word twice and with 2 different meanings.

    e.g. **bit**   *He **bit** too hard on his apple and broke a **bit** off his tooth.*

1.   funny

2.   light

3.   hard

4.   watch

5.   mean

6.   row

7.   even

8.   fine

9.   plain

10.   charge

One word - two meanings (2)

For each of these words, make up a paragraph which contains the word twice and with 2 different meanings.

e.g. **late** *The funeral of the **late** George Sims was on a Friday. His sister was on holiday in Spain at the time. She flew back as soon as she got the telegram and arrived at the church only 5 minutes **late**.*

1. train

2. stand

3. pretty

4. still

5. plant

6. smart

7. over

8. club

9. score

10. down

Link the pictures (1)

A. *Write a short news item that links together these 5 drawings.*

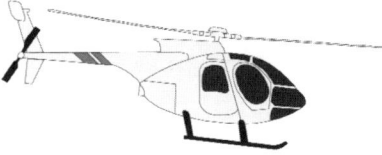

B. *Write a short story that links together these 5 drawings.*

Link the pictures (2)

A. Write a funny story that links together these 5 drawings.

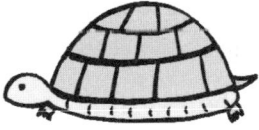

B. Write a report to go on an insurance claim form which links together these 5 drawings.

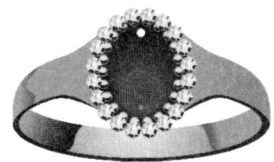

Link the words

Choose one of the circles and make up a short story which includes all the words in it.

A

chips   night   over

petrol   full   sun

B

pop   tube   fan

box   band   star

C

job   place   cash

bottle   offer   question

D

fall   fire   fast

storm   Spring   blow

E

break   Spain

sick   tickets

bags   soon

F

studio   camera   seat

jackpot   bags   soon

microphone   ticket

G

coach   bag

driver   running

door   stand

H

computer   keys

information   wrong

telephone   dentist

Writing advertisements

A. Someone wants to sell this car:

1. Write an advertisement for the car on a postcard to go on the noticeboard of the local supermarket or post office. Make up the details of its history.

2. How would you word an advertisement for the car in the local newspaper, if there was a charge of 30p per word and a minimum of 12 words ?

3. How would the same car be advertised in the newspaper by a car dealer, in a list of 50 cars with only 1 short line per car ?

B. Write a description of this house as it might appear in an estate agent's advertisement.

C. 1. A small jobbing builder wants to place a display advertisement in Yellow Pages. Write down what he might put in it.

2. A recently trained hairdresser wants to place a display advertisement in a local community magazine. She is offering to go to people's homes. Write out a possible advertisement for her.

3. A building society is advertising for a member of staff to work part-time in a local office. Write out what the advertisement might say.

What were they doing ?

Describe these photographs, saying who the group of people might have been, where they were and when the photographs were taken.

Every picture tells a story

1. Write a newspaper headline for the photograph and a caption to go with it.

2. Write a news report on a local event which includes the photograph.

3. Make up a short script for the two people in the photograph to perform on stage.

Fill in the middle

The first and last sentences of some stories and newspaper articles are given below. Complete each one by writing down what happened in between.

1. Andy had 6 T-shirts and 1 pair of jeans. .... The train had gone.

2. May 31st was his birthday. .... It was all over.

3. The queue stretched right round the building. .... The dress was ruined.

4. The alarm clock went off at 5.30 a.m. ....
   .... It could have been worse, she thought, as she drifted off to sleep.

5. The new Chinese Restaurant in the High Street was deserted. ....
   .... " What a day ! " was Lee Wong's only comment.

6. " Where on earth have you been ? " ....
   .... With tears in her eyes, she quietly closed the door.

7. Mr. Charles Pratt, aged 48, a local fisherman, had the surprise of his life today.
   .... That's the long and the short of it.

8. Foreign holidays are on the increase every year. ....
   .... There's sun, sea and sand in Blackpool, too.

What's in store ?

Look at the picture, then answer the questions.

1. On the store indicator board number **6** at the top of the photograph, four of the signs are incomplete. Fill in the missing letters.

2. The sign above the counter on the right of the photograph is incomplete. Fill in the missing letters.

3. What sort of store do you think it is ? Can you name the store ?

4. **a.** Write down what the two sales assistants are saying to each other.

   b. Write down what the man at the counter is thinking.

5. Using the photograph as a starting point, imagine you have been asked to write a week's episodes for a daily 'soap' set in a superstore.

   a. Write down the overall story-line for the week.

   b. Write the story-line for one episode of the 'soap' in detail.

Postcard or letter ?

Messages on postcards are usually brief, with words left out and not always written in complete sentences.

Rewrite each of these messages from holiday postcards as a letter to a friend or relation. Add any extra details you like to make the letter interesting.

1.

Having great time in Brittany. Weather perfect. Camp site brilliant. Kids on beach all day. Good food - and wine ! Back home Saturday, worse luck.

2.

Walking across Ireland. Both have blisters, but getting fit! Coastline amazing - especially the Giant's Causeway. Everyone we meet is very friendly. Stayed in some great places. Only 200 miles to go!

3.

Write your own postcard or letter from Madeira.

MADEIRA

Câmara de Lobos

4.

I'm on holiday in Scotland with Mum and Dad and the baby. It's rained every day and Dad forgot our macs and wellies. The castles are O.K. but we have to go and look at scenery and famous places - really boring. Home tomorrow - can't wait.

5.

Paris in Spring ! Magic ! Eiffel Tower yesterday. Notre Dame today ! Gardens and parks lovely ! Shops out of this world ! Jolies Bergere tonight ! Ooh La La !

Letters of complaint

A. *The letter below was written to Canon about a faulty camera. Rewrite it so that it makes better sense and lay it out correctly, using your own name and address. Address it to: Canon (UK) Ltd., Photo Division, Brent Trading Centre, North Circular Road, Neasden, London NW10 0JF*

```
Dear Canon,

Your Sureshot M doesn't wind on sometimes.  Sometimes
it does and sometimes it doesn't.  Boots says they
won't mend it because I didn't buy it there but they
closed down at Northern Photographic last month after
I bought it there for Christmas.  You've got to repair
it free because it's guaranteed or I want a new one.
You owe me half my holiday photos.

Yours respectfully,
```

B. *Imagine you work in the Customer Services Department of a mail order company, Kitchen Ware Ltd. You receive the letter below.*

Dear Sir or Madam,

re: my order of February 5th

On February 5th, I ordered 2 items from your Catalogue:

    1 Red Slimline Pedal Bin (Ref. 3592/R) £24.00

    1 20cm Omelette Pan (ref. 1784)   £18.95

I enclosed a cheque for £42.95

I received the Omelette Pan within 7 days, with a note saying that the Pedal Bin was out of stock and would be delivered in 7-10 days.

It is now 4 weeks since I ordered. I still haven't received the Pedal Bin and you have cashed the full amount of my cheque.

Your catalogue states that goods are normally dispatched to arrive in 7-10 days. Please let me know, by return, what has gone wrong.

Yours faithfully,

J. Khan (Mrs.)

Write a letter of reply, making up your company's address and the customer's.

Letters to magazines

A. *Many magazines have an 'agony column' in which advice is given to readers who write in with problems about sex, marriage and family matters.*
If you were the 'agony aunt', what would your reply be to this letter ?

Dear Sarah

I don't know what to do. I am 36, married with 2 children and work part-time. My husband and I have been happily married for 14 years but I have just found out that he has been having an affair for the last two years. I am devastated. He doesn't know that I know about it and I don't want to break up our marriage, for the sake of the children. I don't think I could cope on my own anyway, but I just feel that I can't trust my husband any more.

B. *Write a reply to this letter to* **Radio Times***, disagreeing with what the writer says.*

I'm fed up with all the violence, bad language and sex on *EastEnders*. I've watched it for years and it seems to get worse and worse. We live in a so-called working class area of Bristol and we don't see half of the problems that are shown on the TV.

Why can't writers understand that what we want is some good stories about ordinary people which we can really enjoy when we get home from work.

A. P. Smith, Bristol

C. *Write replies to these questions in a newspaper's* **Reader's Queries** *column.*

Why is there always one spoon left in the washing-up bowl after I've drained it ?
Is there a scientific explanation, or is it just sod's law ?

***

Why *Brussels* Sprouts ? Do they come from Brussels ?

***

Which company first introduced the CD and when ?

Formal and informal letters

A letter to an official organisation or a person who is not known to you is written in a different style from a letter to a friend or relation.

Write formal or informal letters, as appropriate, to the people suggested in the situations outlined below.

Examples: *Getting a job*

Dear Mum and Dad,

Great news - I got the job!

Wales, here I come!

More details when I see you at the weekend.

Love

Anne

Dear Sir,

Thank you for your letter of April 21st offering me the post of Receptionist at the Spa Hotel.

I am writing to confirm my acceptance of the post and look forward to starting work on May 22nd.

Yours faithfully,

Anne Nelson

Anne Nelson (Ms)

A. *You and your family are moving to a new house in a few weeks' time. Write to the following people, giving them details about the move:*

1. Your bank manager
2. A close friend or relative
3. A magazine you subscribe to
4. A local club you belong to

B. *Write to the following people telling them about the recent birth of twins:*

1. Grandparents in Australia.
2. An old school friend

C. *A couple expecting a baby and announcing their forthcoming marriage to:*

1. Her parents
2. His parents
3. Her sister
4. His best friend

D. *A couple getting divorced, informing the following:*

1. The building society which holds their mortgage
2. An old friend they haven't seen for some time
3. Their children's school

E. *Informing of the death of a parent:*

1. Parent's brother in Canada
2. Parent's solicitor
3. Electricity company
4. Your closest friend

Make it better

Basic facts are not very interesting to read. They need to be filled out to catch the reader's attention.

A. *Read this example:*

Basic fact
Jack and Carmen went shopping.

Filling it out

- Jack *and **his wife***, Carmen, went shopping.

- Jack ***Robinson*** and his wife, Carmen, went shopping.

- Jack Robinson, ***a tall, handsome man***, and his wife, Carmen, ***a cheerful blonde***, went shopping.

- ***Early one morning***, Jack Robinson, a tall, handsome man, and his wife, Carmen, a cheerful blonde, went shopping.

- Early one morning ***in May***, Jack Robinson, a tall, handsome man, and his wife, Carmen, a cheerful blonde, went shopping ***for a bed***.

Start a new sentence and continue the story.

B. *Fill out the basic facts given in each of the boxes below to make an interesting short story for a magazine or newspaper.*

1.

- The man sat on a bench.

- It was cold.

- It was 2 o'clock.

2.

- I took my driving test today.

- I failed.

3.

- A dog bit a child.

- The child had to go to hospital.

- The parents sued the owner of the dog.

4.

- A bank was robbed.

- Two men were seen running away.

- One man was caught.

- Police are appealing for witnesses.

What's happening ?

Write about the photograph below:

a. As if you were describing it to a blind person.

b. As if you had seen the incident and were telling someone about it on the telephone.

Headlines

Write short newspaper articles to go with some of these newspaper headlines.

BACK
FROM
THE
DEAD

ICE SCREAMS

Gloria and me

CLIFF FALL MOTORIST SEEN BY POLICE

'Kidnap' parrot rescued

It's parking mad!

BEAST
ESCAPES

Dressing for the non-event

Cook's
plea
for the
poor

Forest held
to a point

That'll do nice-Lee

26,000 CUT
IN JOBLESS

Baby nurse dies

A sports report

1. Write a caption for the photograph.

2. Write a short report of about four paragraphs on the soccer match in the photograph, as it might appear in the local paper of the winning side. Give the report a headline.

3. Write a similar report and headline for the match as it might appear in the local paper of the losing side.

4. Imagine that you are the match referee. Write a short report explaining why you booked one of the players in the goal mouth incident shown in the photograph.

Record of personal details

Whenever you fill in a form, you need to give certain details about yourself. It is a good idea to write these out on a sheet of paper and keep it with you to refer to.

The check-list below contains some of the details you need to know.

- Name and address
- Age
- Place of birth
- Family details *(including who you live with, no. of children etc.)*
- Photograph
- Personal appearance and personality
- Schools attended, with dates
- Further education and training schemes, with dates
- Educational qualifications
- Work experience *(full-time or part-time, with dates & reasons for leaving)*
- Periods of unemployment
- Medical history
- Leisure interests, hobbies, sporting record
- National Insurance Number
- Bank account details
- Driving licence, vehicle ownership
- Criminal record

A. *Using the check-list as a guide, write out details about yourself. Add any other information you think would be useful to you.*

B. *When applying for a job, you are often asked to write a **CV (Curriculum Vitae)**. This is a brief outline of your life and experience which gives you the chance to select details that show you are suitable for a particular job.*

Which details from the check-list would you include in your CV if you were applying for the jobs below ?

1. A police constable
2. An advice worker at a drug advice centre
3. A supermarket check-out assistant
4. A plumber
5. An actor
6. A nurse

A mixed bag (1)

1. Imagine you have been asked to make up the questions for a pub quiz. Write down 10 questions on general knowledge, with their answers.

2. Write down directions for someone to follow if they were to walk from the bus station to the swimming pool in a town or city near you.

3. Your grandfather has died and you have organised his funeral.

   a. Write down a timetable to remind you of all the things that will happen on the day of the funeral.

   b. Write out a list of the costs involved.

4. Write down how you would spend £1000 if you won it on the pools or in the Lottery tomorrow.

5. You buy a telephone answering machine for your home.

   Write down the recorded message which you would put on the tape.

6. Listen to a news summary on the radio (if possible, record it so you can play it back).

   Write down in your own words what was the main news item.

7. Listen to a national weather forecast on the radio (record it, if possible).

   Write down what the weather will be for your area.

8. Look up *Sport* on Teletext and find out what the main sports story of the day is.

   Read the full report, then write a few sentences describing the item in your own words.

9. Type an e-mail to a manufacturer requesting more information about a piece of equipment you have bought from them.

10. Write a letter to your local M.P. asking him or her to take some action over an issue which concerns you.

A mixed bag (2)

1. Type an e-mail to TV or radio giving your views on a programme.

2. Write a newspaper review of a television programme or a film you have seen, or a book you have read.

3. Record a short conversation between 2 people.

    a. From the recording, write down the exact words they use.

    b. Rewrite the conversation as it would appear in the script of a play.

4. Record one end of a short telephone conversation (*e.g. in an office, shop, college, school, at home*).

    a. Write out exactly what the person on your end of the telephone says.

    b. Make up the replies of the caller on the other end.

5. a. Write down four different text messages you might send to friends.

    b. Write each message in full, with correct spelling and punctuation.

6. You go to see your 8-year-old daughter in the school pantomime.

    a. Write down what you might say to a friend about the performance.

    b. Write down what you would say to your daughter about it

7. You go to see a play put on by an amateur group. You think that it is a bad play, not very well performed.

    a. A friend in the pub asks you what you thought of it. Write down the actual words you might use in reply.

    b. Write down the actual words you might use in reply if the friend was one of the actors in the play.

8. Write down the reasons why you prefer:

    a. One newspaper to another.   b. One sort of music to another.

9. Write down the arguments for and against one of these:

    a. capital punishment   c. ID cards

    b. privatised railways   d. a single European currency

Index

Acknowledgements

The publishers wish to thank the following for permission to reproduce photographs:

Geoff Prestwich, Blencogo, Wigton, *p.10*; Cumbria County Council Fire Service, *p.17*; Hope's Estate Agents, Wigton, *p.32*; Falcons Touring Cricket Club (Stoke Edith station, Herefordshire, 1912), *p.33*; *Cumberland News*, Carlisle, *pp.34 & 44*; Tesco Photographic Unit, *p.36*; 'A' Flight, 202 Squadron, RAF Boulmer, Northumberland, *p.42*.